Prue

S I M
SAL

and other
GOURMET FOOD

FROM JULIA.

XMAS 2003

Prue Coats
SIMPLY
SALMON
and other
GOURMET FOOD

COLT BOOKS
Cambridge

Colt Books Ltd
9 Clarendon Road
Cambridge CB2 2BH
Tel: (01223) 329059
Fax: (01223) 365866

First published by Colt Books 1995

Text © Prue Coats 1995
Illustrations © Colt Books 1995

ISBN 0 905899 16 4

British Library Cataloguing-in-Publication Data
A catalogue record for this book is available from the British Library

Cover illustration and text illustrations by Kiki Lewis

Printed in Great Britain by Redwood Books.

CONTENTS

INTRODUCTION

Gourmet food always begins with good ingredients and so, of course, that is exactly where this book began. Sophie and Michael Payne, who run a company called Simply Salmon and Other Fine Foods, are constantly being asked for recipes and ways of serving the delicious foods they market. In fact, Sophie got writer's cramp at the trade fairs as she was forever writing out her fail-safe recipes. And so it was decided to produce a book of recipes for everyone who wonders what to cook that is a little different, but easy to prepare, when contemplating salmon and other gourmet food.

When I was asked to compile and write this book I was delighted, as I always enjoy cooking with the best ingredients. I pooled my ideas with Sophie and Michael and their friend Jane Fletcher who used to run a restaurant, and we hope you'll agree we have come up with some stunning recipes.

I have never liked to economize on ingredients, as I consider it to be 'penny wise and pound foolish' to skimp when you are going to spend time and energy on cooking a dish. I do, however, hate waste. 'Left-over' has a stingy, Scrooge-like sound to it so I prefer the expression progessive cookery when I use ingredients that have already been prepared for an earlier dish. For instance, you can cook a whole salmon, buying perhaps a larger one than you would normally contemplate, and with the remaining fish make croquettes or fish cakes, which can then be frozen into a home-made convenience meal.

The majority of the recipes in this book involve salmon one way or another, but what a variety of salmon is available to us all today! Fresh salmon, smoked salmon, hot-roast salmon, gravadlax are all obtainable in supermarkets, and all are represented here. Or you can go one better and order direct from Simply Salmon whose address is in the back of the book. It is also possible to buy superlative cooked hams from Simply Salmon as well as smoked chicken, smoked duck and smoked wild boar, so you will find a fair range of recipes for ham and these special and delicious products together with other gourmet foods like smoked venison, and some game. We have catered for parties, formal occasions and informal barbecues and family meals.

It has been great fun doing this book. My only complaint is that while checking and testing all the recipes I have had to live on an almost exclusive diet of salmon. I now understand why some Victorian domestic staff had it written into their contracts that they were not to be given salmon more than three times a week! However, it was not really a penance, and I hope everyone will find many recipes here that are simply delicious and will become firm favourites when preparing and eating salmon and other gourmet foods.

PRUE COATS

SIMPLY SOUPS

The concept of a salmon soup may come as a surprise, but it can be most delicious. You can have salmon as the main ingredient in a soup that is a creamy, delicate bisque, or a more substantial affair such as a chowder which can serve as a main course for a family supper, or with a spicy oriental flavour to eat chilled for a dinner party. We have included recipes for both hot and cold salmon soups.

SUMMER SOUP
with lettuce, sorrel and smoked salmon

This is an excellent way of using up left-over pieces of smoked salmon and it can be served either hot or cold. The lettuce and sorrel make a delicious soup anyway, and the smoked salmon gives that special touch of luxury.

Serves 6

1 little gem lettuce, finely shredded
110 g/4 oz sorrel
50 g/2 oz butter
1 onion, peeled and chopped
570 ml/1 pint fish stock or vegetable court bouillon

salt and pepper
50 g/2 oz finely chopped smoked salmon
6 thin slices cucumber
6 teaspoons crème fraîche

Melt the butter in a pan and cook the onion and potato until transparent. Throw in the lettuce and sorrel and allow to wilt, then add the stock, cover and simmer until tender. Liquidize and adjust seasoning, then allow to cool. Just before serving and when quite chilled stir in the smoked salmon and pour into bowls. Garnish with a slice of cucumber and blob of crème fraîche. If the soup is to be served hot add the smoked salmon just before serving.

SALMON CHOWDER
with tomato

This is one of Sophie's quick and easy recipes which is ideal for the occasion when someone stays so long for drinks, that rather than break up an enjoyable party you ask them to stay on for supper. As it takes only a short time to prepare and cook, you will only be one, or at the worst, two whiskies or gins worse off!

Serves 6–8

225 g/8 oz cooked salmon
50 g/2oz butter
2 medium onions, peeled and finely chopped
2 large potatoes, peeled and diced
2 x 425 g/15 oz tins chopped tomatoes

570 ml/1 pint water
1 teaspoon sugar
1 teaspoon dried basil
salt and pepper
finely chopped parsley or torn fresh basil to garnish

Melt butter in saucepan, add onion and cook over a moderate heat until soft and transparent. Add the potatoes, tomatoes, water, sugar, basil and seasoning and simmer for 30 minutes. Flake the salmon and stir it in just before serving. Garnish with the parsley or basil.

POTAGE ROSSOLNICK
with salmon balls

It does not take more than a few minutes to make the fish balls but if you prefer you can just add small dice of salmon to the soup 5 minutes before serving and poach gently.

Serves 6–8

Salmon Balls
50 g/2 oz raw salmon
25 g/1 oz fresh white
  breadcrumbs
salt and pepper
1 egg yolk
flour
Soup
1 onion, peeled and
  chopped
25 g/1 oz butter

25 g/1 oz flour
1 litre/2 pints fish stock
2 tablespoons cucumber purée
1 tablespoon celeriac, finely
  diced and blanched
1 tablespoon parsnip, finely
  diced and blanched
1 tablespoon dill pickle, finely
  diced and blanched
1 tablespoon parsley, chopped
2 egg yolks

To make the salmon balls, whizz the salmon, breadcrumbs, seasoning and egg yolk in a food processor until smooth. Take a teaspoon at a time and roll into balls the size of a marble, coat in the flour and refrigerate.

To make the soup, peel half a cucumber, cut into chunks and purée in a food processor until smooth. Melt the butter and sauté the onions until transparent. Sprinkle in the flour and pour in the fish stock stirring constantly. Bring to the boil and simmer for 20 minutes. Strain into a clean saucepan and add 1 tablespoon of cucumber purée, the diced vegetables and parsley. Poach the salmon balls in boiling, salted water for 10 minutes then strain and reserve. Pull soup off the stove, whisk the egg yolks and remaining tablespoon of cucumber purée together, then whisk this mixture carefully into the soup and heat gently. On no account let the soup boil after you have whisked in the egg yolks. Ladle into soup bowls and garnish with salmon balls.

SALMON BISQUE
with diced fennel and Pernod

This is a 'quick cheat' soup which can be made in a matter of minutes provided you have the requisite main ingredients in your store cupboard, and it makes an appetizing start to a summer dinner party.

Serves 4–6

225 g/8 oz cold cooked
  salmon
2 tins lobster bisque
1 pinch cayenne pepper
salt and pepper
1 tablespoon Pernod or dry
  vermouth

1 tablespoon crème fraîche
25 g/1 oz butter
50 g/2 oz fennel bulb,
  finely diced

Whizz the salmon with the lobster bisque, the Pernod (or dry vermouth), crème fraîche and seasonings in a food processor until smooth and creamy, and refrigerate. Melt the butter and cook the fennel until soft and transparent. When cooked stir into the soup. Garnish each bowl with a frond of fennel.

—— SMOKED SALMON SOUP ——
with onion, thyme and soured cream

A n unlikely combination of ingredients, yet they make a
veritable gourmet soup. The crunch of the lightly cooked
onion and the tang of the soured cream offset the richness of
the smoked salmon. If your local emporium does not stock
soured cream, then greek yoghurt can be used instead.

Serves 6–8

225 g/8 oz smoked salmon,
finely chopped
25 g/1 oz butter
25 g/1 oz flour
1 litre/2 pints fish or light
chicken stock

1 onion, peeled and very
thinly sliced
1 pinch dried thyme
1 squeeze lemon juice
salt and pepper
150 ml/¼ pint soured cream
thyme for garnish

Melt the butter, add the flour and cook for a few seconds.
Pour in the stock and stir until smooth. Bring to simmering
point and then add the onion slices, lemon juice and
seasoning. Cook for 5 minutes, the onion should still be
somewhat crunchy. Add the smoked salmon and soured
cream and heat through. Garnish each bowl with a tiny sprig
of thyme.

SPICY SALMON SOUP
with coconut milk

Simply delicious, with a rich texture and a delicately spiced taste. If you are unable to get honey-roast salmon you can use smoked salmon instead. In either case the distinctive smoky taste goes well with the spices and the coconut milk gives a beautifully creamy texture. Serve it well chilled on a hot summer evening and your guests will be clamouring for the recipe.

Serves 4–6

110 g/4 oz honey-roast or hot-smoked salmon, flaked
25 g/1 oz butter
1 shallot, peeled and finely chopped
1 pinch ground cumin
1 pinch ground coriander

25 g/1 oz flour
570 ml/1 pint fish stock
2 tablespoons coconut milk
1 teaspoon sweet mango chutney juice
salt and pepper

Melt the butter and add the shallot, sauté for a few seconds and then sprinkle in the spices. Cook for 1 minute and then add the flour and stir well. Slowly pour in the stock, coconut milk, chutney juice and seasonings until smooth and cook for 5 minutes. Cool, add the flaked fish, adjust the seasoning and refrigerate until required. If the weather turns chilly it is equally good served hot.

STYLISH STARTERS

Hot- and cold-smoked salmon make ideal ingredients for starters and most of the following recipes can be made very quickly, some in a matter of minutes. Even the pâtés don't take long if you have a food processor; the Smoked Salmon Pâté with watercress and fried almonds only took eight minutes when I timed myself, so for the busy person with job and family and with friends to entertain, they are ideal. There is also a recipe for smoked wild boar if you want to start a meal with something completely different.

──SMOKED SALMON PÂTÉ──
with watercress and fried almonds

The fried almonds in this recipe complement the smoked salmon and the crunchiness makes a good contrast with the 'bite' of the watercress. Most of my guests find it very 'more-ish' and you can either serve it as a first course or for a main course at a girls' lunch, accompanied by hot french bread and salad.

Serves 4–6

225 g/8 oz smoked salmon
75 g/3 oz butter
1 tablespoon lemon juice
3 tablespoons greek yoghurt
50 g/2 oz flaked almonds

1 pinch cayenne pepper
½ bunch watercress
50 g/2 oz butter, melted
salt and pepper

Fry the almonds in 25g/1 oz of butter until golden. Whizz the salmon with 50g/2 oz butter, lemon juice, seasoning and yoghurt in a food processor until smooth, then add all (except 6) of the almonds and the watercress and process for a few seconds more. Transfer to a dish, cover with the melted butter and decorate with almonds. Serve with hot toast.

— HOT-SMOKED SALMON PÂTÉ —
with cream cheese and orange

Hot-smoked fish has a more robust flavour than the cold-smoked variety and combines well with cream cheese. For those not brave enough to flavour it with orange juice, just substitute lemon, but it is worth being bold!

Serves 2–4

110 g/4 oz hot-smoked salmon
110 g/4 oz cream cheese
1 squeeze orange juice
1 dash soy sauce
2 drops tabasco sauce
1 teaspoon fresh coriander, chopped
salt and pepper

Put everything in the food processor and whizz until creamy and smooth. Place in a bowl and refrigerate, or serve immediately with rye bread or scandinavian crispbread.

—Sweet & Sour Salmon Pâté—
with hard-boiled egg and dill gherkins

If you have some cold cooked salmon which is not enough for a meal, here is a good example of progressive cookery which makes an excellent start to any meal.

Serves 6

225 g/8 oz cold cooked
  salmon
25 g/1 oz butter
1 tablespoon mayonnaise
1 squeeze lemon juice
2 small dill gherkins,
  chopped

1 teaspoon dried dill
salt and pepper
1 hard-boiled egg,
  roughly chopped

Remove any bones and skin from the salmon and process in a food processor until smooth with all the other ingredients except the egg. Mix this in last but only give a couple of short 'bursts' so that it gives texture to the pâté. Serve with rye bread or pumpernickel.

─── SALMON STUFFED EGGS ───
with lemon mayonnaise

Apart from the time taken to hard-boil the eggs this is one of the quickest starters imaginable and by increasing the quantities could just as easily become the main course for supper in the garden on a hot summer's evening.

Serves 6

110 g/4 oz smoked salmon
  pieces
6 hard-boiled eggs
Lemon Mayonnaise
2 egg yolks
½ teaspoon Dijon
  mustard

275 ml/½ pint sunflower
  oil
lemon juice to taste
1 pinch cayenne pepper
½ teaspoon sugar
salt and pepper

Peel the hard-boiled eggs, cut in half and spoon the yolks into a food processor with the smoked salmon pieces.

To make the lemon mayonnaise, break the uncooked egg yolks into a bowl, add the mustard and slowly drip in the oil while beating with a hand or electric whisk. When the oil is all absorbed add the lemon juice, sugar and seasonings.

Put 2 tablespoons of this mayonnaise into the processor with the yolks from the hard-boiled eggs and smoked salmon pieces and whizz until smooth. Fill the egg halves with the mixture and arrange side by side in ramekins or on small dishes or plates. Spoon over the remaining mayonnaise and decorate with twisted lemon slices. If you are lucky enough to have some in your store cupboard, substitute Payne's Passion for the lemon mayonnaise.

SMOKED SALMON
and avocado cream

This is a real quicky, and the easy availability of the ingredients makes life so much easier for the cook. I can remember when you needed to be Miss Marple or Hercule Poirot to track down either of these two main ingredients, besides which they were terribly expensive. And as for ricotta cheese, the response would have been 'wossat?'.

Serves 4–6

110 g/4 oz smoked salmon pieces
1 heaped teaspoon aspic granules
55 m/2 fl oz boiling water
1 large or 2 small ripe avocado pears

1 110 g/4 oz pot ricotta cheese
1 tablespoon lemon juice
salt and pepper
diamonds of smoked salmon to decorate

Dissolve the aspic in the boiling water. Scoop the avocado flesh into a food processor and add the rest of the ingredients. Whizz until smooth, then spoon into ramekins and decorate with diamonds of smoked salmon. It is best used within an hour or two as the mixture tends to discolour, though you may get away with making it in the morning provided you fill the ramekins to the brim and cover tightly with cling film.

COLD SALMON SOUFFLÉ
and tartare sauce

This light and airy cold soufflé can be used either as a starter, in which case make it in individual ramekins or as a main course for supper. The original wartime recipe included unsweetened condensed milk as a substitute for cream which at that time was in short supply or non-existent. The other ingredient which I have changed is Heinz Salad Cream. I now use Hellmans or any other brand of bought mayonnaise instead. I prefer to make the tartare sauce myself, but if you are short of time then you can just add the shallots, gherkins, capers and herbs to a proprietary brand of mayonnaise.

Serves 6–8

225 g/8 oz cooked salmon
3 egg yolks
150 ml/¼ pint milk
1 onion ring, bayleaf and
  piece of lemon rind
½ garlic clove
6 peppercorns
1 sachet gelatine
2 tablespoons Hellman's
  mayonnaise
1 pinch cayenne pepper
salt and pepper
275 ml/½ pint crème
  raîche, whipped
4 egg whites, stiffly
  whipped

10 g/½ oz aspic granules
275 ml/½ pint boiling
  water
Tartare Sauce
mayonnaise made with
  2 egg yolks and
  275 ml/½ pint oil
1 shallot or spring onion,
  finely chopped
2 gherkins, finely chopped
1 teaspoon capers,
  chopped
1 tablespoon parsley,
  fennel or tarragon,
  finely chopped

Whisk the yolks and milk together in a small bowl, add the onion, bayleaf, lemon rind, garlic and peppercorns and place over a pan of boiling water. Whisk until it thickens, then pull off the stove and fish out the flavourings and discard them. Stir this custard into the salmon with the mayonnaise and seasonings. Dissolve the gelatine over hot water and add to the mixture. When cool fold in the crème fraîche and when it is just beginning to set fold in the egg whites. Make the aspic jelly by dissolving the granules in the boiling water. When cool run it over the top of the soufflé and decorate with slices of lemon.

To make the tartare sauce, make the mayonnaise (see p. 54), then add the remaining ingredients and hand round separately.

If using as a starter serve with buttered granary bread. For a main course serve with a green salad and new potatoes tossed in oil and vinegar and sprinkled with chopped fennel.

—Smoked Salmon Parcels—
with prawns and grapes

This recipe of Sophie's must be one of the quickest, easiest and most delicious starters on record. The combination of tastes and textures is stunning and your dinner party guests will certainly ask for more and beg you for the recipe into the bargain.

Serves 4

175 g/6 oz smoked salmon
175 g/6 oz shelled cooked
  prawns

175 g/6 oz seedless grape
2 tablespoons mayonnaise
  black pepper

Oil 4 ramekins and line with smoked salmon, which should drape over the sides. Mix the prawns and grapes (reserving a few for the garnish) with the mayonnaise and season with black pepper. Spoon the mixture into ramekins, fold the smoked salmon over the top and refrigerate. Loosen the edges with a knife and turn out onto individual plates. Garnish with prawns and grapes.

──Warm Smoked Salmon──
with pepper salad

This is a wonderful recipe for using up old forgotten sides of salmon from the bottom of your freezer. It works better with an unsliced side of salmon as you can cut it thicker than normal but it can also work with thin ready-cut slices. Grilling and skinning the peppers is time consuming and a bit fiddly but the result is well worth it, and this can be done the previous day. It is best to use different coloured peppers and fresh watercress for the contrast of colour and taste.
Serves 8

450 g/1 lb unsliced smoked
  salmon
8 peppers (4 red, 2 green
  2 yellow)
watercress, to garnish
Vinaigrette
1 teaspoon mustard powder
1 teaspoon sugar

1 garlic clove, peeled and
  chopped
salt and pepper
1 tablespoon tarragon or
  wine vinegar
1 teaspoon balsamic vinegar
55 ml/2 fl oz olive oil
55 ml/2 fl oz sunflower oil

Quarter and de-seed the peppers and lay skin-side-up on a grill pan. Grill under medium heat until the skin starts to 'bubble', about 5 minutes. Alternatively you can roast them in a pre-heated oven set at gas mark 9/240°C/475°F. Remove and skin the peppers and cut into thin strips (about 4 from each quarter). Mix with the vinaigrette while the peppers are still warm. Chill until needed.

To make the vinaigrette combine mustard powder, sugar, garlic with vinegars, add oil and stir vigorously.

Pre-heat a griddlepan (frying pan with raised ridges). Slice the salmon into thick chunks about 1cm/½″ thick and 2.5cm/1″ wide. You will need 2 per person. When you are ready to eat, spoon the peppers on to each plate with a generous garnish of watercress. Flash fry the chunks of salmon for about 45 seconds on each side pressing them down with a spatula and serve on top of the pepper salad immediately.

SMOKED SALMON PROFITEROLES
with cheese sauce and prawns

These delicious profiteroles make an unusual starter and can be served hot or cold. If made in mini sizes they can be used as cocktail eats. They also freeze satisfactorily.

Serves 4–6

Choux Pastry
50 g/2 oz butter
150 fl oz/¼ pint water
60 g/2½ oz plain flour,
   sifted
1 pinch dry mustard powder
2 eggs
25 g/1 oz parmesan cheese,
   grated
1 pinch cayenne pepper
salt and pepper
Hot Filling
10 g/½ oz butter
10 g/½ oz flour
150 ml/¼ pint milk
25 g/1 oz grated cheese

1 pinch cayenne pepper
salt and pepper
parsley sauce and prawns
   for garnish
110 g/4 oz smoked salmon,
roughly chopped
Cold Filling
225 g/8 oz cream cheese
110 g/4 oz smoked salmon,
   chopped
1 tablespoon fresh
   coriander, chopped
275 ml/½ pint mayonnaise
   (see p. 54)
1 tablespoon soured cream
   or yoghurt

To make the choux pastry, melt the butter in the water in a pan and when boiling add the flour and mustard all at once and beat furiously off the stove. Add the eggs one by one and continue beating until the mixture leaves the sides of the pan and looks shiny and then add the parmesan and season well. Place dessert spoonfuls on an oiled baking sheet in a pre-heated oven set at gas mark 6/200°C/400°F for 10 minutes and then turn up to gas mark 7/220°C/425°F and continue cooking for a further 25–30 minutes or until golden brown but watch carefully to see they don't burn. This should produce about 18 profiteroles.

To make the cheese sauce, melt the butter in a pan, then add the flour and cook for a few seconds. Then slowly pour in the milk stirring constantly until it thickens. Season well, then add the cheese and smoked salmon. Halve the profiteroles and fill with the mixture. At the last minute pour over some parsley sauce and garnish with prawns.

If the profiteroles are to be served cold make the filling with the cream cheese mixed with the chopped coriander and the smoked salmon. Pour over the mayonnaise into which you have stirred soured cream or yoghurt.

–Melon and Smoked Salmon–
in dill vinaigrette

This starter is delicious served with warm brown rolls or herb bread. It can also be made by substituting prawns and strips of Parma ham for the smoked salmon and scattering them on top of the melon just before serving. Different types of melon work well as the contrasting colours look pretty.

Serves 8

2 melons (different
  varieties)
225 g/8 oz smoked
  salmon cut into strips,
  or trimmings
Dill Vinaigrette
1 teaspoon Dijon mustard

1 teaspoon sugar
salt and pepper
1 tablespoon white wine
  vinegar
2 tablespoons sunflower oil
1 tablespoon fresh dill,
  chopped

Using a melon baller, take all the flesh from the melons. (Alternatively, cut flesh into cubes.)

To prepare the dill vinaigrette, combine all the seasonings with the vinegar and mix well, add the oil and finally the dill and stir together.

Just before serving, add the melon to the salmon, and stir in the vinaigrette. Pile into individual glass dishes or one large dish.

——— TARTARE OF GRAVADLAX ———
with cucumber

This delicious starter can be made just as easily with smoked salmon but the dill flavoured gravadlax gives it a unique flavour. Arranged on individual plates it looks most appealing and whets the appetite in a most satisfactory way.

Serves 4

125 g/4 oz gravadlax, finely diced

50 g/12 oz celeriac, peeled and finely diced

75 g/3 oz cucumber, peeled, de-seeded and finely diced

25 g/1 oz firm tomato, peeled, de-seeded and finely diced

1 spring onion, finely sliced

salt and pepper

1 tablespoon fresh chopped dill

1 teaspoon home-made mayonnaise

1 teaspoon Dijon mustard or 2 tablespoons readymade mustard and dill sauce

greek yoghurt

1 teaspoon toasted mustard seeds

sprigs of dill or fennel

Blanch the celeriac in boiling, salted water for 2 minutes, then drain. Place in a bowl with all the other diced and sliced ingredients and seasoning, and mix gently together with the dill, mayonnaise and mustard or mustard and dill sauce. Oil a 5 cm/2″ pastry ring and sit it on a plate. Spoon in the tartare mixture, cover with a thin layer of yoghurt and smooth. Loosen with a knife and lift off the ring. Repeat on the other three plates. Sprinkle a few toasted mustard seeds on the top and decorate with a sprig of dill or fennel.

The actual tartare mixture can be made the day before and the individual plates arranged an hour or two before you serve your guests.

SMOKED DUCK SALAD
with avocado and raspberry vinaigrette

The raspberry vinaigrette made with wholegrain mustard is particularly good and complements the duck. This is an unusual and attractive gourmet starter for a dinner party.

Serves 4

1 × 225 g/8 oz–275 g/10 oz
  smoked duck breast
mixed leaf salad including
  radicchio chicory
2 avocados
croutons to garnish
  (optional)

Raspberry Vinaigrette
1 teaspoon whole grain
  mustard
2 teaspoons sugar
salt and pepper
1 tablespoon raspberry
  vinegar
3 tablespoons
sunflower oil

Arrange the salad on individual plates. Try to include some radicchio chicory or lollo rosso (red leaved) lettuce for colour. Cut the duck breast diagonally into thin slices. Peel and slice the avocados lengthways and arrange alternately with the duck on top of the salad. There should be about 4 slices of each. Make the vinaigrette and drizzle it over the salad. Garnish with croutons (optional) and serve with brown crusty bread.

SMOKED WILD BOAR
with star anise and Cumberland sauce

Smoked wild boar is a great delicacy and will set your dinner guests talking, especially if you serve it with Cumberland sauce in which you have infused star anise. This oriental spice has a great affinity with all kinds of game to which it imparts a delicate and incomparable flavour.

Serves 4 as a starter or 2 as a main course

225g/8oz smoked wild boar
Cumberland Sauce
1 orange
1 lemon
2 tablespoons redcurrant jelly

75 ml/2 fl oz port or madeira
1 teaspoon dry English mustard powder
1 piece star anise
½ teaspoon ground ginger
salt and pepper

To make the Cumberland sauce, peel the orange and lemon and cut rind into julienne strips. Blanch these strips in boiling water for 5 minutes. Squeeze the juice from the orange and lemon and simmer with the redcurrant jelly, port, mustard, star anise, ginger and seasoning for 15 minutes. Strain, then add the blanched peel and allow to cool.

Arrange the wild boar in overlapping slices on a shallow dish, dribble over the sauce, cover with cling film and leave overnight or for several hours. Serve with chicory salad and warm new potatoes tossed in hazlenut oil and lemon juice.

Easy and Informal Lunch and Supper Dishes

S ome of these recipes are designed for either supper in the garden on a hot evening, when, at the end of the day, you don't want too much hassle, or a cosy lunch or supper in the kitchen when it is freezing outside. Many come under my label of progressive cookery and are useful for making a delectable dish out of something already cooked which is not enough on its own to feed the family again. I have included in this section both cold and hot dishes, incorporating some of the finest ingredients available: smoked salmon, salmon, ham, venison, smoked duck, smoked chicken. The cold dishes are grouped together at the beginning.

TRIPLE SALMON SALAD
with tomato, cucumber, avocado and mozzarella

The combination of colours is most attractive, and for those who are familiar with the classic tricolor salad this fishy alternative makes a nice change. The basil goes very well with the smoked salmon but you could use sprigs of fennel or even coriander instead. If using the latter sprinkle over some crushed coriander seeds as well.

Serves 2–4

110 g/4 oz gravadlax
110 g/4 oz hot-roast salmon (or cold poached salmon)
110 g/4 oz smoked salmon slices
2 large beefsteak tomatoes, thinly sliced
½ cucumber, thinly sliced
1 large or 2 small ripe avocados

125 g/5oz buffalo mozzarella cheese, sliced or 200 g/8oz feta cheese, cubed
1 little gem lettuce
fresh basil leaves and sprigs
best olive oil or basil oil
red wine vinegar
salt and pepper

Have ready a large platter or carving dish. This salad looks nicest on a white one. Roll the smoked salmon and gravadlax slices and arrange the 3 varieties round the perimeter of the dish like the spokes of a wheel. Lay the tomato in a circle of overlapping slices, and then the cucumber. Peel and slice the avocado vertically to make the penultimate circle and end up in the middle with the sliced mozzarella. If you decide to use feta cheese instead, cut this into cubes and pile up in the centre. Decorate with lettuce and basil leaves and dribble on the oil and vinegar, then sprinkle with salt and pepper. Serve with buttered rye bread.

—COLD SALMON POPPADUMS—
with quail's eggs and mayonnaise

This is an adaptation of a dish I had many years ago made with chicken but it is so good that I often make variations, and this one is particularly good. The only stipulation is that you absolutely must spoon the mixture into the poppadums at the last minute or they will go soggy.

Serves 4

225 g/8 oz cooked salmon
275 ml/½ pint lemon
    mayonnaise (see p. 22)
    or Payne's Passion

8 quail's eggs, hard-boiled
    and peeled
4 poppadums
toasted sesame seeds
lettuce leaves to garnish

Boil the quail's eggs for 3 minutes and then peel under running cold water.

Mix the salmon and mayonnaise together. Heat the grill and toast the poppadums until they are crisp and have little bubbles on the surface. Don't turn your back for a minute or you will have a conflagration and set off the smoke alarms. The poppadums should curl at the edges to make a shallow cup. You can, if you wish, shallow fry them but I personally find them too oily done this way. Place one on each plate, fill with the salmon mixture and place 2 quail's eggs on each. Sprinkle with toasted sesame seeds and garnish with lettuce leaves. Serve with a rice and sugar snap pea salad.

─ SMOKED SALMON MUFFINS ─
with soured cream and chives

This is one of Sophie's quickest and easiest supper dishes. Even if your main ingredients are still in the freezer an hour's grace is all you need for the smoked salmon to thaw (in a bowl of water). The muffins can be put straight into the toaster. This dish is also good made with pikelets, scotch pancakes or drop scones, and I have made it with split pitta breads, naan bread or, even once, with chapattis. Fromage frais or greek yoghurt can be used instead of soured cream, though this is best.

Serves 2

225 g/8 oz smoked salmon
4 wholewheat muffins
butter for spreading

150 ml/¼ pint soured
  cream
1 tablespoon fresh chives,
  snipped

Halve and toast the muffins, then spread lightly with butter. Top with the smoked salmon which has been roughly chopped and mixed with the soured cream and chives. If you prefer you can use caviare or black lumpfish roe instead of the chives.

—SMOKED TROUT FISH CAKES—
with crunchy bacon and crushed oatcakes

These fishcakes are best made with home-smoked trout, that is to say in a hot-smoker, but they are also delicious made with fresh trout. The smoky flavour of the bacon goes particularly well and the crunch of the oatcake coating always elicits 'oohs' and 'ahs' from the punters who invariably wonder why they hadn't thought of it themselves.

Serves 2–4

225 g/8 oz cooked trout, smoked or unsmoked
2 rashers smoked streaky bacon
225 g/8 oz mashed potato
1 shallot, peeled and finely chopped
1 tablespoon fresh parsley, finely chopped
1 egg yolk
1 shake Worcester sauce
salt and pepper
flour for dredging
1 whole egg, beaten
crushed oatcakes
fat for frying

Fry the bacon until crisp and crunchy. Flake the fish into a bowl, add the potato, shallot, parsley and egg yolk. Mix well and then crumble in the bacon. Add the Worcester sauce and season well. Scoop out in dessert spoonfuls, roll into balls in the flour, dip in the beaten egg and then coat with the crushed oatcakes and flatten slightly. To crush the oatcakes either give them one or two bursts in a food processor or another easy way is to place them in a sandwich bag and run the rolling pin over them. Fry in bacon fat, if possible, otherwise oil or butter: They freeze well.

MARGARET'S FISH CAKES
with mustard sauce

W hen Michael Payne's mother, Margaret, gave this recipe on Farmer's World one morning the telephone was red hot for days with requests for it. It is simple and simply delicious. You could equally well make these fish cakes with smoked haddock or even any white fish as the mustardy sauce gives the necessary 'lift'.

Serves 3–4

225 g/8 oz cooked salmon
1 tablespoon flour
75 ml/3 fl oz milk
75 ml/3 fl oz fish stock
salt and pepper
25 g/1 oz butter
½–1 teaspoon mustard
  powder

a few drops vinegar
450 g/1 lb mashed potatoes
2 teaspoons chopped parsley
flour for dredging
1 egg, well beaten
breadcrumbs for coating
oil for frying

Blend the flour to a smooth cream with the milk over a low heat. Add the fish stock (or milk if you haven't any stock) stirring constantly until it thickens. Cook for 2–3 minutes and then season with salt and pepper and beat in the butter and the mustard powder blended with a few drops of vinegar. Mix together the mashed potatoes, flaked fish and chopped parsley, then bind with the mustard sauce and adjust the seasoning. Spread the mixture on a plate and allow to cool. Divide into 6 or 8 portions and shape into flat cakes or croquettes. Dredge with flour, coat with egg and breadcrumbs and fry in oil. Alternatively heat some oil in a roasting dish and bake in the oven at gas mark 8/ 230°C/450°F for 15–20 minutes, turning them over half way through cooking.

—— SMOKED SALMON PASTA ——
with cream and lemon

S ophie and Michael took lots of smoked salmon trimmings with them on their skiing holiday and Sophie said this recipe was a life-saver as it fed any number of people, was quick to cook and so delicious that everyone kept asking for more.

Serves 6

450 g/1 lb tagliatelle or any
   other pasta, fresh or dried
225 g/8 oz smoked salmon
   trimmings
25 g/1 oz butter
juice of ½ lemon
275 ml/½ pint double
   cream

salt and freshly ground
   black pepper
fresh grated parmesan
fresh parsley
watercress or lamb's
   lettuce to garnish

Cook the pasta until *al dente* and drain well. Melt the butter in a pan and add the pasta, smoked salmon, lemon juice and half the cream and toss well over a very gentle heat. Season to taste. Add the remaining cream just before serving and stir well. Sprinkle with freshly grated parmesan and garnish with parsley, watercress or lamb's lettuce.

SALMON KEDGEREE
with ginger and lime sauce

Everyone has their favourite recipe for kedgeree. This is mine and if you can't get the ginger and lime sauce, just use a little of the juice from a jar of preserved stem ginger. The sugar snap peas add a bit of 'crunch' and make a good contrast.

Serves 2–4

225 g/8 oz cooked salmon
1 teaspoon sunflower oil
225 g/8 oz basmati rice
2 shallots, peeled and
  finely chopped
boiling water
110 g/4 oz sugar snap
  peas, lightly cooked
1 squeeze lime or lemon juice

2 hard-boiled eggs, chopped
50 g/2 oz butter
1 teaspoon Lea & Perrins
  ginger and lime sauce
  (or other)
2 tablespoons crème fraîche
salt and pepper
1 tablespoon fresh chopped
  coriander

Heat the oil in a saucepan, tip in the rice and coat well. Add the shallots and pour in boiling water to come 2.5cm/1″ above the rice. Cover the saucepan and cook over a very low heat for 15 minutes. Turn off the heat and put a double thickness of kitchen paper over the pan and replace the lid. Leave for 10 minutes. Fork in the salmon and sugar snap peas. Add the hard-boiled eggs, butter, ginger and lime sauce and crème fraîche. Season to taste and sprinkle the coriander over the top.

SALMON CROQUETTES
with capers

These are a family favourite. They are delicious for lunch or supper but are equally at home made in a smaller size as a first course for a dinner party served with a caper hollandaise.

Serves 4–6

225 g/8 oz cooked salmon
60 g/2½ oz butter
60 g/2½ oz flour
275 ml/½ pint milk
1 teaspoon lemon juice
1 shallot, peeled and
  finely chopped
2 teaspoons capers,
  roughly chopped

2 teaspoons parsley, chopped
1 teaspoon anchovy essence
1 pinch cayenne pepper
salt and pepper
2 egg yolks
2 eggs well-beaten
dried breadcrumbs
oil for frying

Melt the butter in a saucepan, then add the flour and cook for a few minutes. Slowly pour in the milk and stir until it thickens, then mix in the salmon and all the other ingredients except the beaten eggs and breadcrumbs. When cool enough to handle, scoop up a dessert spoon at a time, coat in flour and roll into cork shapes. Coat in beaten egg and then in crumbs. Fry in deep fat for 2–3 minutes until golden brown and serve immediately with wedges of lemon, chipped potatoes and green beans.

NOTE: If using a deep fat fryer set it at 190°C/375°F. Monitor the oil temperature in a chip pan with a thermometer if you possess one. Otherwise heat the oil until it is smoking and test by dropping in a small piece of bread crust. If it sizzles to the top and turns brown almost immediately the temperature should be about right.

If serving as a starter with caper hollandaise make the hollandaise in the usual way (see p. 64) and add 2 teaspoons of chopped capers just before serving.

MIXED FISH PIE
with potato and celeriac topping

The mixture of salmon, white fish and shellfish is delicious as the different textures and flavours complement each other. A fish pie to my mind should always have a creamy potato topping, all crunchy and golden where you have made a pattern with a fork, but it can equally well have a puff pastry topping, in which case it can become the main course for a dinner party. This recipe includes celeriac in the potato which goes well with the fish.

Serves 6–8

225 g/8 oz salmon	50 g/2 oz butter
225 g/8 oz haddock or cod	50 g/2 oz flour
6 scallops	2 tablespoons crème fraîche
110 g/4 oz cooked prawns, optional	1 tablespoon fennel, chopped
570 ml/1 pint milk	1 pinch ground nutmeg
1 slice onion	1 pinch cayenne pepper
1 bay leaf	110 g/4 oz celeriac, peeled and diced
1 bouquet garni	900 g/2 lb potatoes, peeled
4 black peppercorns	butter and milk,
salt	salt and pepper

Poach the salmon, white fish and scallops in the milk with the flavourings, then remove to a dish. Make a béchamel sauce with the butter, flour and strained cooking liquor. Stir in the crème fraîche, fennel, nutmeg and cayenne and adjust the seasoning. Add the fish in chunks and the prawns, and spoon into a 1 litre/2 pint pie dish. Blanch the celeriac for 5 minutes and strain. Cook the potatoes, mash and beat into a smooth, creamy purée with the butter, milk and seasoning and then mix in the diced celeriac. Smooth over the fish and make a pattern with a fork. Cook in a pre-heated oven set to gas mark 6/200°C/400°F for 30 minutes or until golden brown. Serve with well buttered chopped spinach and sorrel.

— Ham and Spinach Soufflé—

Spinach and ham are a perfect marriage as this recipe demonstrates. Ideally your guests should be sitting, knives and forks at the ready. Oven temperatures vary and you can never be absolutely sure of cooking times, 5 minutes either way.

Serves 4–6

175 g/6 oz cooked ham, minced	1 teaspoon made English mustard
75 g/3 oz frozen chopped spinach, thawed	1 teaspoon tomato ketchup
50 g/2 oz butter	1 good pinch grated nutmeg
50 g/2 oz flour	salt and pepper
75 ml/½ pint milk	4 egg yolks
5 g/1 oz parmesan cheese, grated	5 egg whites
	butter
	fresh breadcrumbs

Melt the butter and add the flour. Cook for a few seconds, then add the milk, stirring constantly and cook until the mixture leaves the sides of the pan. Mix in the ham, spinach, ketchup, nutmeg and seasonings and then beat in the egg yolks. You can prepare to this point in advance.

Butter a 1.5 litre/2½ pint soufflé dish and coat with crumbs. This gives a crunchy coating and makes it easier for guests to help themselves without the soufflé sticking to the sides of the dish. Beat the egg whites until stiff and fold into the soufflé mixture. Spoon into the dish and cook in the centre of a pre-heated oven set at gas mark 6/200°C/400°F for 30–35 minutes. Serve immediately.

HAM PATTIES
with mustard sauce

This recipe is an excellent way of using up the end of a ham joint. The mustard sauce is a most delicous accompaniment. It is a kind of mustardy hollandaise. The patties can also be frozen and used as a quick convenience meal.

Serves 6–8, makes approxiamately 18 patties

225 g/8 oz ham
450 g/1 lb potatoes
50 g/2 oz butter
1 onion, peeled and
  finely chopped
Worcester sauce
110 g/4 oz grated cheese
1 tablespoon fresh parsley,
  chopped
salt and freshly ground
  black pepper
flour
1 egg, beaten

fresh breadcrumbs
sunflower oil and butter
  for frying
Mustard Sauce
1 egg
55 ml/2 fl oz water
55 ml/2 fl oz wine vinegar
2 tablespoons granulated
  sugar
1 tablespoon mustard
  powder
5 g/½ oz butter
salt

Peel and cook the potatoes, mash them well and transfer to a bowl. Sauté the onion in butter until soft, process the ham until finely chopped and add both to the potato together with the Worcester sauce, cheese, parsley and seasoning. Mix well and leave to get cold. Take a tablespoon at a time and roll into balls in the flour. Dip in the beaten egg, coat with the breadcrumbs, flatten into cakes and fry in a mixture of sunflower oil and butter.

To make the sauce, liquidize all the ingredients for 10 seconds, then cook in a small pan over a very low heat until thick and smooth – it should look like custard. Do not allow it to boil or the eggs will become scrambled. Hand round separately and warn your guests to be cautious as it is rather hot.

──── SMOKED CHICKEN PLAIT ────
with apple

An excellent dish for a family supper or for a friendly kitchen lunch. The apple and smoked chicken go beautifully together. If you don't have any of the smoked variety this recipe can be made with plain cooked chicken and some time ham.

Serves 6

225 g/8 oz smoked chicken, diced
425 ml/¾ pint milk
50 g/2 oz butter
50 g/2 oz plain flour
1 small red pepper, diced
½ bunch salad onions, chopped
450 g/1 lb Bramley cooking apples, peeled and chopped
4 tablespoons fresh seeds chopped parsley

4 tablespoons fresh chopped parsley
salt and ground black pepper
450 g/1 lb packet chilled puff pastry
1 egg, beaten
1 tablespoon sesame or poppy seeds

Place the milk, butter and flour into a pan and heat, stirring continually until sauce thickens. Add the pepper, onions, apple, parsley and seasoning. Allow to cool and then mix in the chicken. Roll out the pastry to form a rectangle approximately 32 cm/13″ x 28 cm/11″. Spoon the chicken mixture down the centre of the rolled out pastry. Make 6 to 8 cuts along the two longer sides of the pastry and fold over alternate strips of pastry to form a plait effect. Brush with the beaten egg, decorate with sesame or poppy seed and bake in a pre-heated oven set at gas mark 5/190°C/375°F for 35 minutes until golden brown. Serve with brown rice and sugar snap peas.

— SMOKED CHICKEN CRUMBLE —
with cucumber

The cucumber makes an unusual addition to this bake. If you don't have smoked chicken you can use ordinary cooked chicken, but the smoking does give a special and unusual flavour.

Serves 2–4

1 smoked chicken
1 onion, peeled and
  chopped
50 g/2 oz butter
50 g/2 oz flour
425 ml/¾ pint milk

1 teaspoon whole grain
  mustard
salt and pepper
1 cucumber
4 tomatoes
110g/4oz grated cheese
110g/4oz breadcrumbs

Remove the meat from the chicken and cut into chunks. Fry the onion in the butter, sprinkle in the flour and cook for 1 minute. Slowly add the milk stirring constantly until the sauce thickens, then mix in the mustard and chicken and season to taste. Peel the cucumber, halve lengthways and de-seed. Cut into 1cm/½" slices and add to the sauce, then pour into an ovenproof dish. Slice the tomatoes and lay on top and finally sprinkle on a mixture of the cheese and breadcrumbs. Bake in a pre-heated oven set at gas mark 5/ 190°C/357°F for 30 minutes.

SALADE CAUCHOISE
with ham and potato

I first came across this ham and potato salad just after the war when I was in Normandy visiting stud farms in connection with my job at the British Bloodstock Agency. It is an excellent way of stretching a small quantity of ham and is definitely an example of progressive cookery. The best potatoes to use are Charlotte, Belle de Fontenay, Ratte or Pink Fir Apple, which are varioiusly obtainable in supermarkets when they are in season.

Serves 2–4

450 g/1 lb salad potatoes
225 g/8 oz cooked ham
225 g/8 oz centre and inner stalks of celery
275 ml/½ pint crème fraîche
150 ml/¼ pint single cream
1 tablespoon wine vinegar
juice of ½ lemon
salt and pepper

Cook the potatoes in their skins and peel them when cool. Cut into 4 cm/1½" x 2 cm/1" batons. Cut the ham and celery into julienne strips. Whip the crème fraîche and add the single cream, vinegar, lemon juice and seasoning. Mix everything together gently, taking care not to break the potatoes.

Serve in an attractive bowl with hot french bread.

HAM MOUSSE
with cream and mustard

If you are short of time this is very easy to make and if you cool the serving dish in the fridge or freezer it will set in no time at all. Tasty and popular with all ages.

Serves 10

450 g/1 lb cooked ham
4 tablespoons hot water
¾ chicken stock cube
   sachet gelatine
190 ml/⅓ pint single cream
pepper

1 tablespoon mustard
   mixed with a splash of
   lemon juice
425 ml/¾ pint double
   cream, whipped
3 egg whites, stiffly
   whipped

Put the hot water into a basin over a pan of hot water. Add the stock cube and sprinkle over the gelatine. Allow to soak and dissolve. Whizz the ham, single cream, mustard and lemon juice and pepper in a blender, then pour in the gelatine mixture. Allow to cool then fold in the double cream and finally the egg whites. Turn into a serving dish, then place in the fridge to set.

This recipe can also be made with smoked salmon instead of ham. Replace the mustard with 1 pinch of ground nutmeg.

——Smoked Venison Platter——
with red onion and apple jam

Smoked wild venison is now widely available. Accompanied by the red onion jam it makes a delicious and unusual meal. It is worth making several pots of the jam as it also goes beautifully with smoked wild boar or duck breasts. Other excellent accompaniments are Cumberland sauce (see p. 33) or raspberry vinaigrette (see p. 32).

Serves 2–4

225 g/8 oz smoked wild
  venison
Red Onion and Apple Jam
700 g/1½ lb red onions
225 g/8 oz cooking apples,
  peeled and chopped
225 g/8 oz granulated sugar

1 teaspoon salt
1 tablespoon olive oil
275 ml/½ pint red wine
  vinegar
150 ml/¼ pint port
4 juniper berries, crushed
ground black pepper

To make the jam, heat the oil gently in a saucepan. Peel the onions, cut in half and then into thin crescents. Tip into the saucepan with the apple, sugar and salt. Cover tightly with a lid and cook very slowly for about an hour. Add the vinegar, port, juniper berries and pepper and cook uncovered until shiny and syrupy. Spoon into heated jars and cover.

Divide the venison slices amongst 4 plates. Garnish with a spoonful of the jam and serve with wild rice.

OCCASIONAL OCCASIONS

You're giving a party and need inspiration? All the recipes in this section are ideal for impressive occasions, and would make a good centre-piece for a cold buffet or a special picnic for Glyndebourne, Ascot or Speech Day.

SALMON TERRINE
in three contrasting layers

This recipe is designed to be made with hot and cold
smoked salmon or trout, but if you can't lay your hands
on the hot-smoked variety just use poached salmon or trout
for the top and bottom layers. The layers look wonderful
when sliced, and the combination of tastes and textures is
sensational. Well worth the effort.

Serves 4–6

5 g/½ oz aspic dissolved in
55 ml/2 fl oz boiling water
4 thin slices lemon
Court Bouillon
bones from 450 g/1 lb salmon
275 ml/½ pint water
150 ml/¼ pint white wine
1 onion and 1 carrot, peeled
    and cut up
1 piece celery
1 bay leaf
3 peppercorns
1 piece lemon peel
25 g/1 oz aspic granules
Layer 1
110 g/4 oz hot-smoked or
    poached salmon
1 heaped teaspoon
    horseradish sauce
2 tablespoons jellied
    court bouillon

salt and pepper
1 tablespoon crème fraîche
Layer 2
110 g/4 oz packet smoked
    salmon
2 tablespoons chopped fresh
    dill
1 pinch cayenne pepper
1 teaspoon lemon juice
2 tablespoons jellied court
    bouillon
Layer 3
110 g/4 oz hot-smoked
    or poached salmon
2 tablespoons greek yoghurt
2 teaspoons capers (or finely
    diced cucumber)
2 tablespoons jellied court
    bouillon
salt and pepper

Pour the plain dissolved aspic when cold, into a 570 ml/
1 pint oiled loaf tin and allow to set. Lay the lemon slices
down the middle. Make a court bouillon with the first 8
ingredients and simmer for 30 minutes, then add the salmon
for layer 1 and layer 3 and poach for 6 minutes. Or smoke

it. Skin and divide flesh into two bowls. Strain the court bouillon and bring to a fast boil, sprinkle in the aspic and stir until dissolved. Allow to cool to a syrupy consistency.

Layer 1. Flake the fish and mix in the horseradish and jellied court bouillon and seasoning then fold in the crème fraîche. Spoon into the tin and put in the fridge.

Layer 2. Cut the smoked salmon into small dice and and mix in the dill, cayenne and lemon juice and lastly the jellied court bouillon. Spoon into the tin and spread evenly.

Layer 3. Flake the fish, mix with all the ingredients and spoon into the tin. Cover with cling film and leave to set.

Turn out and serve with buttered pumpernickel or rye-bread.

POACHED SALMON
Russian style

A ll the Baltic states have salmon rivers and a distinctive cuisine, none more so than Russia. The following recipe is particularly suitable for farmed salmon and it makes a change from the usual cucumber covered pink torpedo beloved by British caterers.

Serves 6–8

11.35 kg/3 lb salmon
575 ml/1 pint fish stock
1 bottle white wine
150 ml/¼ pint sweet
  pickled gherkin juice
1 leek, finely chopped
50 g/2 oz button mushrooms
5 shallots, peeled and
  chopped
¼ celeriac peeled and
  chopped
3 gherkins, chopped
salt and pepper
parsley, chopped
1 hard-boiled egg, chopped
Mayonnaise
2 egg yolks
½ teaspoon Dijon mustard
½ teaspoon sugar

2 tablespoons olive oil
275 ml/½ pint sunflower oil
2 teaspoons wine vinegar
salt and pepper
Russian Salad
1 kg/2 lbs potatoes
225g/8oz carrots
110g/4oz parsnip or turnip
110g/4oz celeriac
110g/4oz French beans
110g/4oz mange-tout peas
½cucumber, de-seeded
  and diced
1 x 150g/6oz tin sweetcorn
570ml/1pint mayonnaise
salt and pepper
1 tablespoon dill, chervil
  and parsley, chopped

Place the fish on the grid in a fish kettle together with the stock, wine, gherkin juice, mushrooms, shallots, celeriac, gherkins and seasoning. Bring to the boil, skim well and simmer gently for 10 minutes. The water should just 'shiver'. Allow to get cold in the court bouillon, then transfer fish to a serving platter and remove the skin. Strain the vegetables and tip into the food processor with 1 tablespoon of the cooking liquor. Give 2 sharp "bursts" to chop roughly, mix in the parsley and hard-boiled egg and pour over the fish.

To make the mayonnaise, place the yolks in a basin, add the mustard and sugar and slowly pour in the oil drop by drop to begin with and then in a steady stream, beating constantly with a wire whisk or electric hand beaters until it is really thick. You may have to use more oil to get the right consistency. Finally add the vinegar, salt and pepper.

Serve the salmon with the mayonnaise and Russian salad, made as follows. Cook the potatoes and cut into 2.5 cm/1″ dice. Cut the carrots and parsnips or turnips into 2.5cm/1″ dice and cook in lightly salted water for 5 minutes; they should still be slightly crunchy. Cut the beans and mange-tout into 5cm/2″ lengths and cook for 2-3 minutes. Allow to cool and mix everything together with the mayonnaise. Adjust the seasoning and serve in a bowl with the chopped herbs sprinkled on top.

SALMON EN CROÛTE
with asparagus and cream

When there is a special occasion and you need to feed large numbers of people, this delicious recipe can be made in advance and put into the oven about 35 minutes before you want to serve it. The asparagus and creamy filling set off the richness of the salmon and the pastry keeps it all moist with the full flavour of salmon and asparagus retained. It can be eaten hot or cold. Most fishmongers and fish departments in supermarkets will fillet the salmon, removing the main bone, skin, head and tail. This leaves only the tiny bones which are a bit fiddly to extract, but not too difficult. When cooked, this dish is very dense so should be served in thin slices.

Serves 10–12

2 × 900 g/2 lb salmon
   fillets
900 g/2 lb fresh asparagus
   or 2–3 tins
275 ml/½ pint cream
2 teaspoons dill, chopped
10 wafer thin slices ham
   (optional)

450 g/1 lb packet puff
   pastry
2 egg yolks
2 tablespoons milk
salt and pepper

Cook the asparagus and drain. Rub through a sieve or whizz in the food processor. If using tinned asparagus, drain and use all the asparagus. Blend in the processor with the cream and season to taste with salt and ground black pepper. Roll the pastry out into 2 large rectangles on a floured surface. The piece for the top should be slightly larger, and it's easier to check the size if both are rolled out at the same time. Place one rectangle of pastry on the greased baking sheet and spread a layer of cream and asparagus purée down the middle. Place one of the fillets of salmon on the asparagus purée, sprinkle with some of the chopped dill, and cover with more asparagus purée. Place the second fillet on top with the thick end over the thin end of the first fillet to make an even sandwich. Sprinkle on more chopped dill and spread on more purée. Cover with the remaining pastry rectangle. Press down the edges to seal. Decorate with leaves or fishes from the left-over bits of pastry and make a couple of slits for steam holes. This can now be refrigerated for several hours – if your fridge space allows – until you are ready to cook it.

One bit of advice: this is a large and heavy object, and not very forgiving, so it is wise to make it straight on to the greased baking tray so that you do not have to lift the pastry parcel, thus avoiding the chance of its disintegrating.

When you are ready to cook the salmon, mix the egg yolks with the milk and brush on to the pastry. Place in a pre-heated oven set at gas mark 7/220°C/425°F for 10 minutes and then lower the heat to gas mark 6/190°C/375°F and bake for a further 25 minutes, when the pastry will be golden brown. Serve with new potatoes and crisp green salad. Any remaining asparagus and cream purée can be handed round as a sauce.

SMOKED CHICKEN
and cranberry ring

Smoked chicken is generally used as a starter or in salads but it lends itself very well to this creamy ring. The sharpness of the cranberries makes a good contrast of taste. It looks very decorative, and can be the focal point of a buffet.

Serves 4–6

meat from 1 smoked chicken
275 ml/½ pint well reduced
 stock made from the chicken
 carcass
50 g/2 oz butter
50 g/2 oz flour
salt and pepper

50 g/2 oz cranberries
1½ sachets gelatine
55 ml/2 floz dry sherry
275 ml/½ pint crème
 fraîche, whipped
fresh coriander or parsley
 for garnish

Whizz the smoked chicken roughly in a food processor. Melt the butter, sprinkle in the flour and cook for a few seconds. Pour in the stock stirring constantly until smooth and simmer for 10 minutes, then add the chicken meat and season with salt and pepper. Simmer the cranberries in a tablespoon of water until soft but not squashy and stir gently into the mixture. Soak the gelatine in the sherry until it has swelled and then dissolve over hot water. Stir into the chicken and sauce. When cool fold in the crème fraîche and spoon into an oiled 850 ml/1½ pint ring mould. Turn out and garnish with sprigs of coriander or parsley and serve with a green salad.

— CELEBRATION SMOKED CHICKEN —
with mango dressing

This really is an original combination and becomes the talking point of any celebration buffet, be it a christening, anniversary or wedding. The mango dressing gives a luxury touch and looks most appetizing.

Serves 8–10

2 x 1.2 kg/2½ lb
  smoked chickens or
  700 g/1½ lb smoked
  chicken and 700 g/1½ lb
  smoked ham
5 level tablespoons fresh
  coriander, finely chopped

2 bunches spring onions,
  trimmed and chopped
1 large cucumber
2 large ripe mangoes
3 limes
275 ml/½ pint sunflower oil
salt and pepper

Cut the chicken into 5cm/2″ chunks, discarding the skin and bones and place in a bowl with the coriander and spring onions. Peel the cucumber, cut in half lengthways and remove seeds with a teaspoon. Slice diagonally and then leave to drain on kitchen paper for about 30 minutes. Cut down either side of the mango stone, cut away the flesh from the skin and place in a food processor with the grated rind and the strained juice of the limes. Process until smooth and then with the motor still running add the oil in a slow, steady stream. Pour mixture over the chicken, season to taste, cover and refrigerate for up to a day. Mix well before serving.

QUICK JAMBON PERSILLÉ
and Swedish potato salad

The original recipe for this Burgundian dish includes pigs'
trotters and involves clarifying the stock. The former are
difficult to get and are probably not the modern cook's
favourite ingredient, and the whole palaver is altogether too
time consuming. This is my lazy version and with its
sparkling jelly you can serve it as a dinner party main course
in the summer. Marmalade cured ham makes it even more
delectable.

Serves 4–6

450 g/1 lb cooked ham
  or marmalade cured
  ham, cut into chunks
2 tins chicken consommé
150 ml/¼ pint white wine
2 shallots, peeled and finely
  chopped
1 sachet gelatine
1 tablespoon white wine
  vinegar
salt and pepper
4 heaped tablespoons
  parsley, chopped

Swedish Potato Salad
900 g/2 lbs cooked new
  potatoes, sliced
3 tablespoons pickled
  beetroot, finely chopped
1 tablespoon capers
2 tablespoons each fresh
  parsley, chervil and tarragon,
  chopped
6 tablespoons best olive oil
1 tablespoon wine vinegar
salt and pepper
1 tablespoon leek or spring
  onion, finely shredded

Simmer the consommé, wine and shallots for 20 minutes and
then strain. Soak the gelatine in the vinegar and when it has
swelled, dissolve over a pan of hot water, then add to the
consommé and leave to cool. Season with salt and pepper.
Toss the ham chunks in the parsley and place in a bowl or
dish. A white one is nicest as it shows off the pink of the ham
and the emerald green of the parsley. When the liquid is just
beginning to turn syrupy pour it carefully over the ham. If
the parsley all floats to the top wait until the jelly is just

beginning to set and stir very carefully. Serve with watercress salad and Swedish potato salad.

To make the Swedish potato salad, put the potatoes, which should still be warm into a bowl. Sprinkle the beetroot, capers and herbs over the top then pour over the oil and vinegar and season. Garnish with the shredded leek or spring onion.

FROM BARBECUE TO BUFFET

The hot dishes in this section can be eaten informally, barbecue style, at a dinner party or as part of a buffet. Some of the best food in the world is included in the ingredients, except game which follows in a separate section. Some of dishes, for instance the Double Crust Salmon Tart or the Salmon en Croûte, can be served cold as well as hot and would also do for those special occasions in the previous section.

— MARINATED SALMON FILLETS —
with honey and ginger

Served with basmati and wild rice and mixed salad, this makes a quick and unusual main course.

Serves 4–6

6 salmon fillets
2 tablespoons sunflower
  oil
50 g/2 oz butter
Marinade
5 tablespoons olive oil
5 tablespoons Worcester
  sauce

5 tablespoons runny
  honey
1 × 1 cm/½″ cube ginger,
  grated
salt and pepper
3 tablespoons fresh
coriander, chopped
½ bunch spring onions,
  chopped

Mix the marinade ingredients in a non-metallic dish. Add the fish, turn it over in the marinade and leave for 3 hours in the freezer covered with cling film. Heat the oil and butter in a frying pan until very hot. Add the fillets and fry over a very high heat for 2–3 minutes on each side. The outside should be black and crispy and the inside pink and moist.

Whole Baked Salmon
with watercress hollandaise

For those who get in a tizzy when faced with having to cook a whole salmon, this method is really easy and also avoids the necessity for a fish kettle. The watercress hollandaise gives a good colour contrast as well as providing a 'tangy' taste.

Serves 10–12

1 whole salmon	2 teaspoons lemon juice
sprigs of fennel or dill	110 g/4 oz–175 g/6 oz
lemon slices	unsalted butter cut
salt and pepper	into dice
melted butter	salt and pepper
Watercress Hollandaise	ice cubes (optional)
3-4 egg yolks	1 tablespoon blanched
2 teaspoons white wine	and chopped watercress

Lay the fish on a well-buttered sheet of foil in a roasting dish. Salt and pepper the stomach cavity and fill with fennel sprigs and lemon slices. Seal the foil and make into a loose parcel. Don't make it too tight or the steam won't be able to circulate. Pre-heat the oven to gas mark 5/190°C/375°F and cook for 8 minutes per each 450 g/1 lb.

To make the watercress hollandaise, put the egg yolks, wine and lemon juice in a bowl and place over a pan of hot, but not boiling, water. Whisk in the butter bit by bit until the sauce thickens. Season, stir in the chopped watercress and pour into a warm (not hot) sauce boat. If the sauce looks like curdling while you are making it, pull the pan off the stove and add an ice cube.

NOTE. Don't use very fresh eggs and don't take them straight out of the fridge.

—PAN-FRIED SALMON ESCALOPES—
with lemon butter and braised lettuce

Mauro Bregoli of the Manor House Restaurant, Romsey gave me the following mouthwatering recipe for escalopes of salmon which will earn you at least 3 michelin stars from your friends. The great plus of this recipe is the ease and speed with which you can astonish your guests when you produce it in a matter of minutes.

Serves 6

6 salmon escalopes
butter for frying
6 little gem lettuce
25 g/1 oz butter

Lemon Butter
110 g/4 oz unsalted butter
juice of 1 lemon
salt and pepper

Heat the 25 g/1 oz butter in a saucepan and sauté the lettuces until they start to brown. Cover tightly, shake and cook over a very low heat for 5 minutes. Melt the remaining butter in a thick frying pan until foaming and then flash fry the eascalopes; a bare 30 seconds on each side will be sufficient. Transfer to a warm serving dish.

To make the lemon butter, heat the lemon juice, pull the pan off the stove and beat in the unsalted butter in small pieces until it has melted, then add the seasonings. Pour over the escalopes and serve straight away.

SALMON METROPOLE
with capers

Salmon escalopes are best for this dish as they can be rolled up, and smoked salmon alternating with the escalopes makes it especially delicious.

Serves 4

4 salmon escalopes	salt and pepper
4 smoked salmon slices	275 ml/½ pint single
1 teaspoon capers	cream
50 g/2 oz butter	crushed cornflakes

Butter a shallow gratin dish liberally. Roll up the salmon escalopes and smoked salmon slices and lay them side by side in the dish, then sprinkle with the capers. Season well and pour the cream over the top. Sprinkle on a thick layer of crushed cornflakes, dot with butter and bake in a pre-heated oven set at gas mark 6/200°C/400°F for 20–30 minutes. Serve with new potatoes and fine green beans.

WOKKED SALMON
with fresh ginger and orange

Another 'quickie'. Strange as it may seem, the combination of ginger and orange goes remarkably well with the salmon, and the mangetout peas provide the contrasting 'crunch-factor'.

Serves 2

225 g/8 oz salmon,
  cut in thin strips
1 tablespoon sunflower
  oil
225 g/8 oz mangetout
  or sugar snap peas
4 spring onions, sliced
  in rings

5 g/½ oz fresh ginger,
  finely chopped
soy sauce
juice of 1 orange
sesame oil
sesame seeds

Cut the pea pods in half. Heat the oil in a wok and throw them in. Shake and stir and cook for 2–3 minutes. Add the spring onions, stir and push up the sides of the wok. Throw in the salmon strips and ginger and shake around for barely 1 minute. Shake in a good dollop of soy sauce, pour in the orange juice and reduce until syrupy. Add a dash of sesame oil and sprinkle some seeds over the top. Serve with brown rice.

GRILLED SALMON STEAKS
with sauce Bercy, tomatoes and capers

I f unexpected guests have arrived, and you are stuck for a main course and have some salmon steaks in your fridge or freezer they can be quickly cooked and given an added zest with the sauce Bercy, tomatoes and capers.

Serves 2–4

4–6 salmon steaks
butter for grilling
Sauce Bercy
50 g/2 oz shallots, peeled
 and finely chopped
275 ml/½ pint dry white
 wine
50 g/2 oz tomatoes peeled,
 de-seeded and finely diced

1 tablespoon capers, rinsed
 and drained
juice ½ lemon
salt and pepper
2 tablespoons finely chopped
 fresh dill
110 g/4 oz unsalted butter

To cook the salmon steaks heat the grill and put butter in the pan. When it is foaming slip in the steaks and coat on each side. Cook for 4 minutes on each side, then transfer to a warm serving dish.

To make the sauce, simmer the shallots in the wine until it has reduced to 55 ml/2 fl oz. Add the tomato and cook for a few minutes, then tip in the capers and lemon juice and season with salt and pepper. Heat through, then draw pan off the stove and whisk in the butter in little pieces. Sprinkle in the dill and pour the sauce over the steaks.

— BARBECUED SALMON STEAKS —
with tarragon sauce

A delicious main course for supper in the garden on those hot summer evenings, and easy for the chef supervising the barbecue while everyone else is milling around.

Serves 6

6 salmon steaks
3 tablespoons olive oil
juice of 1 lime
1 tablespoon fresh
  tarrragon, snipped
Tarragon sauce
275 ml/½ pint single
  cream

50 g/2 oz softened butter
1 teaspoon flour
3 egg yolks
salt and ground black pepper
1 tablespoon fresh tarragon,
  chopped
juice of 2 limes

Brush the salmon steaks well with the olive oil and lime juice, and sprinkle with the tarragon. Grill over a hot barbecue for 2-3 minutes on each side and serve at once with the tarragon sauce.

To make the tarragon sauce, process the cream, butter, flour, egg yolks, salt and pepper. Transfer to a heatproof bowl and set it in a pan of simmering water which should come halfway up the sides of the bowl. Stir the sauce occasionally with a wire whisk as it cooks. It should take just over half an hour to thicken. Just before serving stir in the tarragon and lime juice.

— DOUBLE CRUST SALMON TART—
with tarragon and lemon

This delectable double crust tart will surprise and delight your guests who won't be expecting this filling. It can also be eaten cold and makes a gourmet addition to any *al fresco* meal such as Glyndebourne or Ascot. It freezes well.

Serves 4–6

450 g/1 lb salmon
2.25 litres/4 pints water
1 tablespoon tarragon
    vinegar
1 onion
1 carrot
1 bay leaf
2 bouquet garni
½ lemon
50 g/2 oz butter
1 shallot, peeled and finely
    chopped
50 g/2 oz flour
800 ml/1½ pints fish stock

1 piece lemon peel
juice of ½ lemon
1 tablespoon fresh,
    chopped tarragon
salt and pepper
Pastry
225 g/8 oz self-raising flour
1 egg, well beaten
pinch salt
150 g/5 oz block margarine
1 egg, well beaten
1–2 tablespoons water
1 egg beaten for painting
    pastry

Bring the water, vinegar, vegetables, herbs and ½ lemon to the boil and simmer for 20 minutes. Lower in the piece of salmon, bring back to simmering point and poach for 8–10 minutes. Transfer to a bowl and strain the stock. Skin and debone the salmon, and set aside. Melt the butter and sauté the shallot for 1 minute. Add the flour, cook for a few seconds, then pour in the stock and stir until it is smooth and has thickened. Add the lemon peel, juice and tarragon and finally the salmon which you have skinned and deboned. Stir well to break up the fish, adjust seasoning and allow to cool.

Make the pastry and when it has rested for 30 minutes roll it out, reserving one-third for the lid. Line an 18cm/7″ oiled flan dish and spoon in the salmon mixture, heaping it in the middle. Moisten the edges and cover with the remaining pastry. Make a couple of slits, decorate, and paint with beaten egg. Cook in pre-heated oven set at gas mark 6/200°C/400°F for 10 minutes then lower heat to gas mark 4/180°C/350°F for a further 30 minutes. As the pastry is very crumbly it is best to let it sit for 10 minutes so that it is easier to cut. Serve with new potatoes and spinach.

SALMON PANCAKES
with wild mushrooms

Salmon has a great affinity with mushrooms and particularly the wild ones. Luckily for those living in towns, most supermarkets sell shitake and oyster mushrooms fresh and you can also buy the dried porcini in packets.

Serves 2–4

225 g/8 oz salmon, cooked
  and flaked
25 g/1 oz butter
1 shallot, peeled and finely
  chopped
25 g/1 oz oyster mushrooms,
  cut in strips
25 g/1 oz shitake mushrooms,
  chopped
25 g/1 oz flour

150 ml/¼ pint milk
2–3 drops balsmic vinegar
150 ml/¼ pint single
  cream
1 pinch cayenne pepper
salt and pepper
Pancake Batter
110 g/4 oz plain flour
2 eggs, well beaten
275 ml/½ pint milk
1 tablespoon sunflower oil

Melt the butter and sauté the shallot and mushrooms until cooked but not browned. Sprinkle in the flour, stir well and add the milk, the balsamic vinegar and half the cream. Season well and mix in the salmon.

With the batter mix make 8 pancakes and divide the salmon mixture between them. Roll up and lay on a shallow fireproof dish. Spoon over the rest of the cream and flash under a hot grill until golden and bubbling. Serve with sauté potatoes.

SALMON KEBABS
with onion and peppers

E asy to prepare, and the marinade can be made well in advance. Ideal for the barbecue as well as for cooking under the grill.

Serves 4–6

900 g/2 lb skinless salmon
  fillet
6 tablespoons olive oil
3 tablespoons lemon juice
2 tablespoons dry white wine
4 tablespoons fresh parsley,
  finely chopped

2 medium onions, quartered
2 green peppers, cut into
  pieces
salt and pepper
lemon wedges to garnish

Mix the olive oil, lemon juice, wine, parsley and seasoning in a non-metallic bowl. Cut the fish into 2.5cm/1" cubes and add to the marinade. Separate the layers of onion, lay over the fish and leave in a cool place covered for at least an hour. Pre-heat the grill to high. Thread cubes of fish onto skewers alternating with pieces of onion and pepper. Brush skewers with marinade and grill for 1–2 minutes. Turn heat to medium and cook for a further 4–5 minutes on each side, brushing with more marinade. Garnish with lemon wedges.

── BAKED RAINBOW TROUT ──
and asparagus

Rainbow trout are available from most supermarkets and fishmongers and the large ones can make a good substitute for salmon when you have a quantity of people to feed.

Serves 6–8

1 large rainbow trout
softened butter
juice of ½ a lemon
salt and pepper
1 bundle of asparagus tips
2 hard-boiled egg yolks,
  sieved

1 tablespoon fresh parsley,
  chopped
110 g/4 oz butter
50 g/2 oz fresh white
  breadcrumbs

Place the whole fish on a large sheet of well-buttered foil. Pour on the lemon juice, season with salt and pepper and make into a loose parcel. Place in a pre-heated oven set at gas mark 5/190°C/375°F and bake for 8 minutes per 450g/1 lb. When cooked transfer to a warmed serving dish and drizzle over the cooking juices.

Cook the asparagus tips in boiling, salted water for 3–4 minutes or steam them for 5 minutes. They should still be bright green and slightly crunchy. Don't on any account do as a friend of mine does and cook them until they are khaki colour! Use them as a garnish for the fish.

Sprinkle on the sieved egg yolks and parsley, or you can use a whole chopped hard-boiled egg if you prefer. Heat the butter and fry the crumbs in it until golden, then pour the sizzling mixture over the fish just before serving. Plain boiled potatoes and spinach go well with this dish.

FLAMING CRAYFISH
and shallots

When we first came to live in Hampshire, friends had a stretch of chalk stream and from early August crayfishing parties were held. The crayfish were hauled out in their home-made traps which had previously been baited with pieces of kipper. A camp fire was built and the crayfish were plunged into boiling salted water, cooked and eaten in the fingers with thick slices of bread and butter and copious swigs of alcohol. Now we can buy crayfish with relative ease in the supermarket, and what a gourmet meal they make, especially when cooked in the following way.

Serves 4–6

30 crayfish	1 pinch powdered bayleaf
2 shallots, peeled and finely chopped	1 pinch dried thyme
	salt and pepper
120 g/5 oz butter	1 heaped teaspoon cornflour
75 ml/3 fl oz brandy	1 tablespoon chopped parsley
570 ml/1 pint white wine	

Sauté the crayfish with the chopped shallots in the butter (use more if needed). Pour over the warmed brandy and set alight. When the flames have died down add the wine, sprinkle on the herbs and seasoning, cover and cook over a high heat for 10 minutes. Arrange the crayfish on a dish and keep warm. Reduce the wine by fast boiling and add a heaped teaspoon of cornflour mixed with water and stir until it thickens. Pour this sauce over the crayfish and sprinkle with chopped parsley. Serve with hot French bread and don't forget the finger bowls! If you don't have some handy, use soup bowls filled with water and a lemon slice in each.

──── SMOKED DUCK BREAST ────
with ginger, lemon and honey sauce

Y ou can serve this hot or cold equally well but if you decide on the former be extremely careful to just 'flash-fry' the pieces of duck as they have already been cooked by the smoking process and should still be faintly pink.

Serves 2–4

2 smoked duck breasts
butter or oil
4–6 tablespoons ginger
   and honey juice
juice of ½ lemon
lemon wedges to decorate

Ginger and Honey Juice
110 g/4 oz preserved stem
ginger
150ml/¼ pint syrup
2 tablespoons runny honey

To make the sauce, pulverize the ginger in a food processor, or liquidize. Add the syrup from the jar from the preserved ginger and the honey and continue whizzing until really smooth.

Cut each duck breast vertically in two. Melt the butter in a frying pan and pour in the sauce. Add the lemon juice and cook until it starts to caramelize. Toss the pieces of breast in it until well coated and then arrange on a dish and pour over the sauce. Decorate with lemon wedges and serve with purée of potato and celeriac if the smoked duck breasts are to be eaten hot, or with a fennel and walnut salad if to be served cold. It is best to sauté duck breasts in oil if they are to be eaten cold as butter congeals.

HAM GOUGÈRE
with sun-dried tomatoes

This makes an excellent main course dish for a dinner party and is an ideal way to make a small amout of cooked ham go a long way.

Serves 4–6

225 g/8 oz cooked ham, cut into chunks
570 ml/1 pint milk
1 bayleaf
1 onion ring
1 small garlic clove, peeled
50 g/2 oz butter
50 g/2 oz flour
50 g/2 oz cheddar cheese, grated
1 teaspoon made English mustard
6–8 sun-dried tomatoes in oil
1 teaspoon dried oregano
salt and pepper
double quantity of choux pastry (see p. 28)

Bring the milk to the boil with the bayleaf, onion and garlic and allow to infuse for 10 minutes. Melt the butter, add the flour and cook for a few seconds, then add the strained milk, stirring until thick. Add the cheese, mustard, sun-dried tomatoes, oregano, seasoning and ham and set to one side.

Make the choux pastry as per the recipe on p. 28 but instead of making individual puffs place dessertspoons of the mixture on a buttered baking tray in the form of a circle and bake in a pre-heated oven set at gas mark 6/200°C/400°F for 10 minutes then increase the heat to gas mark 7/220°C 425°F for a further 30–35 minutes until golden brown. Transfer the ring to a serving dish, fill with the ham mixture and heat in the oven for 3–4 minutes. Serve with spinach and new potatoes.

GOURMET GAME

Gourmet is the operative word with game, especially if it is cooked well. Most supermarkets now stock a wide selection and so these treats are no longer confined to the sporting brigade and their friends. I have selected some of my favourite recipes for partridge, pheasant, pigeon, wild duck and venison for this section and although guinea fowl and quail are not strictly game, they fall into this category as far as gourmet food is concerned. Some of these recipes can be prepared in advance and finished off at the last minute. All can be enjoyed informally or can grace the smartest dinner party table.

WILD DUCK
with orange and cranberries

Wild duck, particularly mallard, are a delicious treat. It is advisable to cut off the parson's nose and preening gland to avoid a fishy taste. For perfection they should be covered with salt and left in a cool airy place for 24 hours with an onion in the body cavity. Oranges and cranberries are used in both cooking the birds, and making the sauce, and in a compôte which is served separately.

2 mallard
1 orange
2 tablespoons cranberries
   or redcurrants
1 tablespoon flour
1 glass sherry
50 g/2 oz butter

150 ml/¼ pint stock
ground black pepper
Compôte
juice of 2 oranges
225 g/8 oz cranberries or
   redcurrants
sugar to taste

Prepare the birds as above and just before you want to cook them remove the onions and brush off the excess salt. Pepper the insides and stuff each one with a long strip of orange peel (without pith), half an orange and 1 tablespoon cranberries. Pre-heat the oven and set at gas mark 7/220°C/425°F and melt the butter in a roasting pan until foaming. Put in the birds, baste well and roast for 45 minutes to 1 hour. Scrape the stuffing into the roasting pan, then transfer birds to a warmed serving dish and keep warm.

To make the sauce, squash the orange and cranberries with a potato masher to extract the juice, then remove them with a slotted spoon. Turn up the heat until bubbling on top of the stove and pour in the sherry. Cook for a few seconds, then add the stock and pour over the ducks. Garnish with orange slices and serve with braised fennel, sauté potatoes and the compôte.

To make the compôte, cook the cranberries in orange juice and sugar to taste and allow to cool. Cut the oranges into segments and mix together with the cranberries. Hand round separately.

PHEASANT SAUSAGE
with leek and lemon sauce

T his unusual pheasant recipe can be eaten either hot or cold and will earn you 'brownie points' from your guests, not least those who don't like to deal with bones.

Serves 4–6

1 pheasant	110 g/4 oz sausage meat
1 onion, carrot and stalk of celery	1 egg
	flour to dredge
2.25 litres/4 pints water	dried breadcrumbs
bouquet garni	butter for frying
salt and pepper	*Leek and Lemon Sauce*
25 g/1 oz fresh white breadcrumbs	6 baby leeks or 3 large ones
	1 tablespoon water
2 tablespoons milk (approx)	1 tablespoon lemon juice
1 shallot peeled and finely chopped	2 egg yolks
	50 g/2 oz unsalted butter
10 g/½ oz butter	salt and pepper
110 g/4 oz butter	

Remove the flesh from the pheasant and weigh out 225 g/ 8 oz. Put the carcass in a saucepan with the vegetables, water, herbs, salt and pepper, and simmer for 1½ hours. Soak the breadcrumbs in milk. Cook the shallot. Squeeze out the breadcrumbs and add to the shallot together with the egg and whizz until really smooth. Transfer to a bowl and chill while the stock is cooking. When this is ready strain it into a shallow pan. Take tablespoonsful of the pheasant mixture and roll gently into sausage shapes in the flour. Lift with a slotted spoon and lower into the gently boiling stock and poach for 20 minutes. Remove and cool slightly, then roll in the breadcrumbs and sauté in the butter until brown. Keep warm on a dish in a low oven.

For the sauce, cut the leeks, if small, into 10 cm/4″ lengths and cook with the water in a tightly covered pan over a low heat for 8–10 minutes – they should be cooked but not sludgy. (If using large leeks cut into rounds and cook for only 5 minutes.) Heat 1 tablespoon each of the leek water and lemon juice in a pan, pull off the heat and whisk in the egg yolks. Add salt and pepper to season. Add the butter in little pieces until it has melted. Garnish the sausages with the cooked leeks and for a main course serve with broccoli and pasta shapes, and hand round the sauce separately.

If using as a starter, place 1 sausage on each individual small plate and garnish with leek and a spoonful of sauce.

To eat cold just remove from the poaching water and roll in finely chopped parsley. Serve with lemon mayonnaise (see p. 22). If you wish to freeze the sausages, do so before rolling them in the breadcrumbs.

PARTRIDGE RISOTTO
with wild mushrooms

I am besotted with wild mushrooms and it always annoys me that the British are so dismissive of these marvellous 'freebies'. Fungi have a natural affinity with game, none more so than ceps (*Boletus edulis*) or Penny Buns as they are known in English. They go particularly well with partridge and pheasant. Fresh ones are best, if you can find them, or you will have to make do with dried porcini, the Italian equivalent, which you can find in most supermarkets. Failing this use oyster mushrooms.

Serves 2

2 young English or French
    partridges
25 g/1 oz butter
1 shallot finely chopped
275 ml/½ pint stock
Risotto
1 cup arborio rice

275-425 ml/½-¾ pint
    stock
110 g/5 oz ceps or 1 packet
    dried porcini
25 g/1 oz butter
2 tablespoons cream
salt and pepper

Brown the partridges in the butter with the shallot and transfer to a casserole dish. Season and pour in the stock. Place in a pre-heated oven set at gas mark 6/200°C/400°F for 10 minutes, then reduce the heat to gas mark 4/180°C 350°F and cook for a further 45 minutes or until tender.

Cut the ceps into cubes and fry in the second lot of butter for a few minutes, then remove with a slotted spoon to a plate. Tip the rice into the same pan and stir round so that it is all coated, then add a little stock and stir. Keep adding stock every so often and let the rice cook until it is absorbed. Carry on doing this until the rice is soft, then stir in the ceps and the cream.

Pile the risotto on to a dish, sit the partridges on top and pour over the juice from the casserole. This is true gourmet fare.

——— BRAISED GUINEA FOWL ———
with star anise and vermouth

Guinea fowl is widely available in supermarkets and provides an excellent alternative to game. As it tends to be dry the best way is to braise or to cook it in a clay chicken brick. The following is a recipe dreamed up by my daughter and the combination of star anise and the vegetables makes the bird succulent and moist and gives it an unusual flavour.

Serves 2

1 guinea fowl	1 star anise
50 g/2 oz butter	salt and pepper
1 onion, peeled and diced	150 ml/¼ pint vermouth
1 parsnip, peeled and diced	150 ml/¼ pint single cream

Brown the guinea fowl and vegetables in the butter and transfer to a casserole. Place the star anise beneath the bird, season well with salt and pepper and pour in the vermouth and cream. Place in a pre-heated oven set at gas mark 4/ 180°C/350°F and cook for 1 hour. Baste occasionally. Transfer to a heated serving dish, surround with the vegetables and pour over the sauce. Serve with buttered carrots and sauté potatoes.

If you are going to cook it in a chicken brick, simply place the vegetables and star anise in the bottom of the brick, oil the bird and sit it on top. Add the vermouth and cream and place in a cold oven. Switch on and set at gas mark 9/ 240°C/475°F and leave for 1½ hours. This cuts out the frying so is good for the health conscious. This method will produce more juice so you may find it necessary to reduce the liquid by fast boiling.

QUAIL ITALIANO
with cream cheese and prosciutto

I frequently see people peering at quail on my local supermarket shelves and clearly they are wondering how to cook
them. These little birds are hardly enough for a hungry
person so you need to make them a bit more filling. The
cream cheese and prosciutto help to do this and, in addition
it is a good idea to sit them on a thick piece of fried bread.
Many people stuff them with grapes but I prefer to give the
fruity contrast by mixing diced melon into the chicory salad.

Serves 2

2 quail, oven ready
225 g/8 oz cream cheese
½ teaspoon each dried
  thyme and rosemary
salt and pepper
4 slices prosciutto or parma
  ham
110 g/4 oz butter
1 glass marsala
275 ml/½ pint brown sauce

1 galia, charentais or ogen
  melon
Brown Sauce
butter for frying
1 carrot, onion and leek
  peeled and chopped
570 ml/1 pint rich game
  stock
1 sprig each fresh parsley,
  thyme and marjoram

To make the brown sauce fry the vegetables in the butter
until brown, add the stock and herbs and simmer for 1 hour.
Strain and press well to extract all the juice from the
vegetables. Skim off the fat, then reduce by fast boiling to
275 ml/½ pint. This can be made ahead of time and frozen.

Mix together the cream cheese, herbs and seasoning and
spoon into the body cavities of the quail. Cover the breasts
of the birds with the slices of prosciutto and fix with cocktail
sticks. Melt the butter in a roasting tin until foaming and put
in the birds, breast down. Place in a pre-heated oven set at
gas mark 6/200°C 400°F and roast for 30 minutes. Take the
birds out of the oven and place on a warm dish. Add the
marsala to the pan and then the brown sauce and reduce to

about 150 ml ¼ pint. Sit the quail on thick slices of fried bread and pour over the sauce.

Peel and de-seed the melon and cut into cubes, then mix into a chicory salad dressed with a lemon vinaigrette. Serve with tagliatelle.

PIGEON BREAST SALAD
with hazelnut dressing

This can either be a main dish or a starter, in which case halve the number of pigeon breasts. The fennel and hazelnut oil complement the pigeon particularly well.

Serves 4

8 pigeon breasts
oil for sauteeing
1 avocado pear
1 bulb fennel
1 packet toasted, chopped
 hazelnuts

Dressing
2 teaspoons lemon juice
1 teaspoon Dijon mustard
1 teaspoon honey
2 tablespoons hazelnut oil
salt and pepper
chopped hazelnut to garnish

Sauté the pigeon breasts in the oil for 2 minutes on each side and allow to get quite cold. Slice very thinly lengthways and arrange in a fan on individual plates. Garnish with quarters of peeled avocado and chopped fennel.

Mix the dressing (add more lemon juice if necessary) and dribble it over each plate, then sprinkle with chopped hazelnuts. Serve with very thin slices of buttered rye bread.

MEDALLIONS OF VENISON
with blackberry sauce

This is quick and easy recipe. The medallions can be marinated and then put in the freezer. Take them out 1 hour before you need them and they will be ready to cook.

Serves 6

6 medallions cut from the loin 5cm/2" thick
best quality olive oil
1 clove garlic, peeled and finely chopped
2 shallots, very finely chopped
110 g/4 oz butter

110 g/4 oz blackberries (cranberries or bilberries can be substituted)
275 ml/½ pint very strong reduced stock
2–3 drops balsamic vinegar
1 pinch ground cloves
salt and pepper
6 crisply fried croûtons

Marinate the medallions overnight in the olive oil and garlic covered tightly with cling film. Sauté the shallots in 25 g/ 1 oz of the butter, add the blackberries, stock, vinegar, cloves and seasoning and cook for 5 minutes or until the fruit is soft, then remove some berries for decoration. Reduce the sauce to half, then whizz in the processor. Press through a sieve to eliminate the pips. Add a little brown sugar if it tastes tart. Sauté the medallions in the remaining butter, about 3–4 minutes on each side. Place one on a croûton on each plate. Pour the sauce round and decorate with berries. Dribble a little cream (soured if possible) round. Serve with sauté potatoes and lightly braised celeriac or glazed kohl rabi.

PRETTY AND TEMPTING PARTY FOOD

I hardly need say that for preparing eats for a drinks party, smoked ingredients are the hostess' greatest ally and can be used for a variety of quickly made 'nibbles'. The salmon pinwheels and smoked salmon and cream cheese rolls can be made well ahead and then frozen and only need half an hour to thaw. The pastry cases can also be put in the freezer and filled at the last minute and are the only faintly fiddly item on the cocktail party agenda. Otherwise its all pretty simple and very gourmet.

—SMOKED SALMON PINWHEELS—
with cheese and chives

I find this recipe extremely useful for parties since it can be made a week or two in advance and left in the freezer. It is also a delicious starter when served with a mixed salad leaf garnish and brown bread and butter.

Serves 25 as a canapé or 10 as a starter

450 g/1 lb smoked salmon
400 g/14 oz cream cheese
1–2 tablespoons fresh chives
    or dill, snipped

milk, if necessary
freshly ground black pepper

Beat the cream cheese until a soft spreading consistency is reached, adding milk as necessary. Stir the chosen herb and pepper into the mixture. Lay out the smoked salmon in a single layer on pieces of cling film to produce two rectangles measuring approximately 30cm/12″ × 45cm/18″. Spread the cream cheese mixture over the salmon and cut the rectangles in half widthways with a sharp knife to create four 30cm/12″ × 23cm/9″ rectangles. Using the cling film to help you, roll the salmon into a swiss roll shape 30cm/12″ wide. Wrap the rolls in cling film and freeze until firm. Slice into 1cm/½″ slices with a sharp knife. If the pinwheels are set out on a serving dish, they take about half an hour to defrost.

SMOKED SALMON ROLLS

These popular delicacies are easily put together and make a little smoked salmon go a long way. You can prepare them a day in advance and wrap them in cling film. They can then be sliced into rounds just before serving.

1 thin brown sliced loaf	450 g/1 lb smoked salmon
1 packet butter	lemon wedges to garnish

Roll out each slice of bread firmly with a rolling pin. Butter them, then using a sharp knife remove the crusts. Lay the smoked salmon on the bread, using a butter knife to stretch the salmon. Roll them into rolls and lay seam side down on a plate until ready to serve. Cut into 1 cm/½″ rounds and serve with lemon wedges.

QUAIL'S EGG DELICACIES

Quail's eggs rolled in smoked salmon

Quail's eggs are particularly delicious and if you hard-boil them for 5 minutes and peel them under cold running water they are then ready to be wrapped in smoked salmon. Secure each one with a cocktail stick and arrange them on a dish or platter. In the centre have two small ramekins one containing celery salt and the other cayenne pepper.

Stuffed quail's eggs

If you have a great deal of patience another mouth-watering canapé can be made by halving the hard-boiled quail's eggs, then stuffing them with a mixture of the yolks puréed with smoked salmon, cream cheese and lemon juice. The best way to fill them is with a forcing bag.

—— Pastry Case Fillings——

Pastry cases can be made with left over short crust pastry in the form of tiny tartlets or boat shaped barquettes. Small vol-au-vents can be made from frozen puff pastry. Alternatively you can buy ready made cases of all kinds from supermarkets.

Suggested fillings

Cream cheese and smoked salmon garnished with lumpfish roe.

Tiny bits of smoked salmon, 1 seedless grape and 1 prawn on thick mayonnaise (see Smoked Salmon Parcels with prawns and grapes p. 26).

Smoked chicken with cranberry jelly.

Smoked wild boar chopped and mixed with star anise flavoured Cumberland jelly (see p. 33).

Creamy cold scrambled egg with black pepper and chopped smoked salmon.

Smoked Salmon Profiteroles

These can be made with the choux pastry recipe (see p. 28) but use two coffee spoons to make the profiteroles and fill them with cream cheese and smoked salmon using a forcing bag.

Bits on Sticks

Smoked chicken balls

These can be made in exactly the same way as the pheasant sausages (see p. 80) but using smoked chicken instead. Make up a half quantity and using a teaspoon roll them in flour into ball or tiny cork shapes. Poach and allow to get cold, then roll in finely snipped chives. Impale on cocktail sticks. Serve with a very lemony mayonnaise.

Smoked trout and oatcake

Take equal quantities of hot-smoked trout and cream cheese and mix well together. Add 1 or 2 crisply fried bacon rashers crushed up, season well, roll into balls and coat with crushed oatcakes.

Spreads and Pâtés

Small squares of sesame crispbread, mini french toasts, rounds of pumpernickel all make good 'carriers' for the following spreads:

Smoked salmon, almond and watercress, (see p. 19).

Hot-smoked salmon pâté, with cream cheese and orange, (see p. 20).

Salmon pâté with hard-boiled egg and gherkin, (see p. 21).

Granary toast rounds or cocktail biscuits spread with a mixture of ham, mustard, Worcester sauce, tabasco and butter whizzed in the food processor.

DIPS

The imagination can run riot as there are so many wonderful combinations. Here are some ideas, using many of the recipes and food suggestions found earlier in this book.

Chunks of smoked duck to dip into mayonnaise flavoured with raspberry vinegar and whole grain mustard.

Chunks of smoked duck to dip into ginger, honey and lemon sauce (see p. 76).

Assorted vegetable batons to dip into Paynes Passion or thick mayonnaise flavoured with bits of salmon.

Wholemeal 'Scooples' with a dip made of gravadlax, fromage frais, dill and mustard.

Sesame sticks with a dip made of houmus whizzed up with smoked chicken.

Celery batons with a dip made of taramasalata whizzed up with some smoked salmon pieces.

INDEX

Simply Salmon is run by Michael and Sophie Payne. Michael has been in the food industry for 14 years starting with a year on the family Salmon farm based at Ardvar in Sutherland. Here he developed his love and interest in salmon which led him to wholesaling to London's top hotels and restaurants from 1982 to 1991.

In 1991 **Simply Salmon** was formed after Michael was asked to promote a new brand of smoked salmon called *Scottish Eagle*. This was based on the Ardvar salmon being smoked in the traditional way by a small smokehouse at Grantown-on-Spey. Every side of salmon is individually hung in the old-fashioned brick kilns and smoked over oak chippings thereby ensuring *Scottish Eagle*'s unique quality so hard to find in these days of mechanical kiln smoking.

Scottish Eagle was then 'tried and tested' by the *BBC Good Food Magazine,* where it was praised for its 'delicate complex flavour which is very appealing with a clean lingering smokiness' and subsequently took first place. **Simply Salmon** became the trading company for *Scottish Eagle* and enabled Michael once again to join forces with his father at Ardvar to make it a family business.

In 1992, **Simply Salmon** expanded into the mini hamper market, mainly due to the requests of customers who wished to add 'a little bit more' to their smoked salmon gifts.

Simply Salmon is still very much a family run company and great care is taken with all customers. There is now a wide range of products including salmon, smoked salmon, smoked chickens, smoked duck, smoked wild boar, smoked venison sausages, wild boar terrine en croûte, pâtés, kippers and so on. Everything is available by mail order either through the post or delivered by overnight carrier and 90 per cent of products can be frozen. If you would like a price list for the full range of products please ring:

Simply Salmon

Severals Farm, Arkesden, Saffron Walden, Essex CB11 4EY
Tel: 01799 550143 Fax: 01799 550039